COMBINING CHEMICALS

FUN CHEMISTRY BOOK FOR 4TH GRADERS

CHILDREN'S CHEMISTRY BOOKS

BABY PROFESSOR
EDUCATION KIDS

Speedy Publishing LLC
40 E. Main St. #1156
Newark, DE 19711
www.speedypublishing.com

One of the key aspects of chemistry is the ability to combine various substances. Sometimes these combinations might cause the chemicals to react and bond creating a totally different substance which is known as a compound. Occasionally there may be no bonding or reaction, and this is known as a mixture of the combined substances. Read further to learn about different types of mixtures, reactions, and bonding.

Tap water

MIXTURES

A mixture results when more than one substance combine, although not chemically.

The properties include the following:

- components can be easily separated.
- they retain their original state.
- and the components' proportions can vary.

Smoke results from the mixture of particles when suspended in air. Tap water results from a mix of water and various other particles.

Homogeneous and heterogeneous are the two main categories of mixtures. When all substances distribute evenly through the mixture it is considered to be homogeneous (air, blood, salt water).

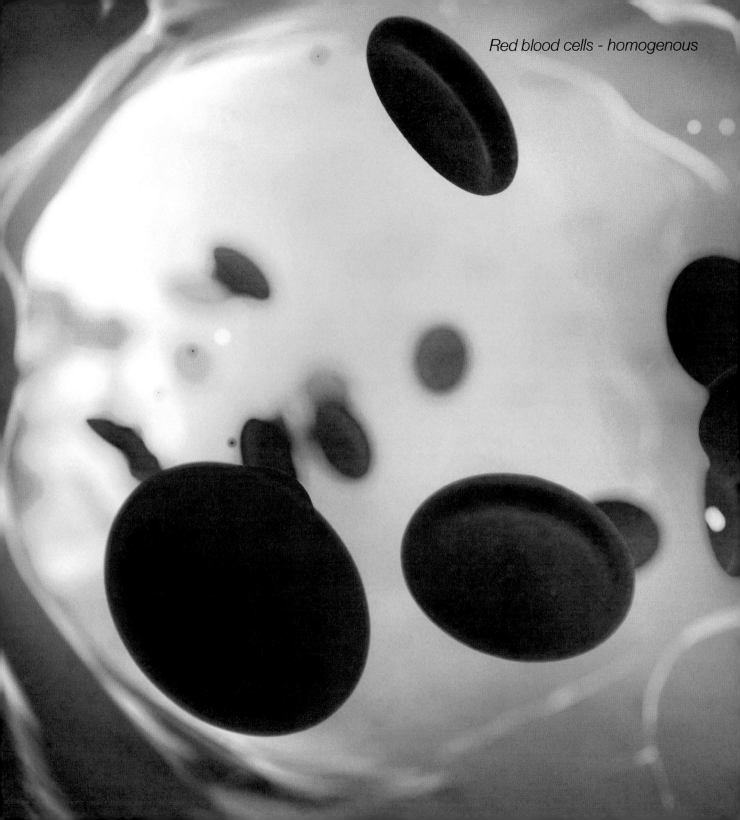

Red blood cells - homogenous

When the substances do not distribute evenly through the mixture, it is known as a heterogeneous mixture (rocks, chocolate chip cookies, pizza). There are more specific types of heterogeneous and homogeneous mixtures listed below.

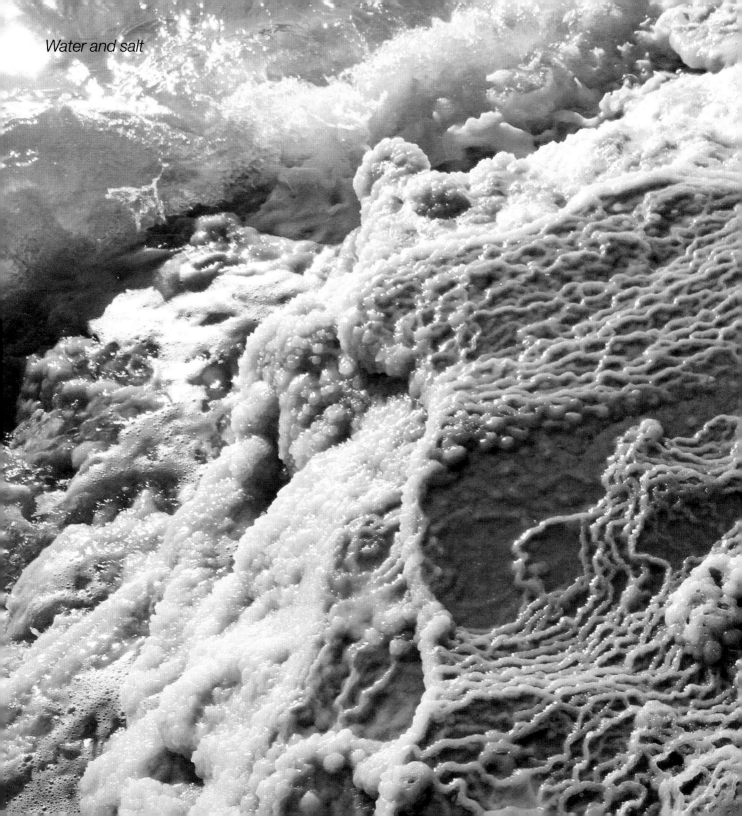

Water and salt

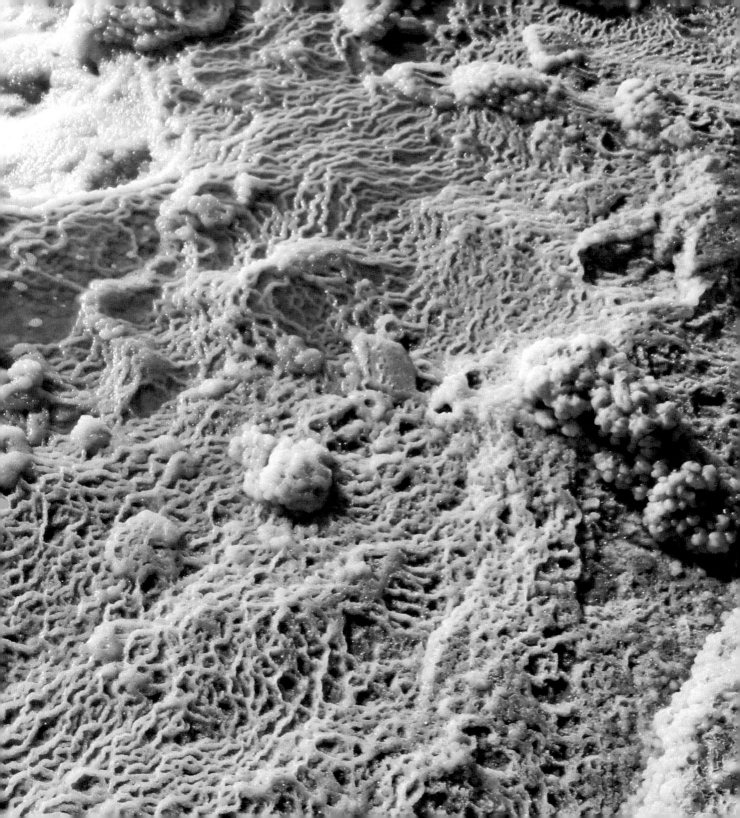

SOLUTIONS

Solutions are homogeneous and are made up of a mixture where one of the substances dissolves into another substance.   The solute is the dissolving substance and the solvent is the non-dissolving substance.

A perfect example of a solution is salt water. While the components are able to separate easily by evaporation they each retain their properties in their original state. When the salt is dissolved into the water and you no longer see it, it is evenly distributed into the water, with water being the solvent and salt being the solute.

WHAT IS THE DIFFERENCE BETWEEN A SOLUTION AND A MIXTURE?

In the world of chemistry, a solution is essentially a form of mixture that is uniform throughout. Think about the salt water discussed earlier. This is known as a "homogenous mixture." If a mixture is not uniform throughout, it is not a solution. Think about sand in water. This is referred to as a "heterogeneous mixture."

Cold rolled steel coil at storage area in steel industry plant.

ALLOYS

Alloys are homogeneous and are comprised of a mixture of elements that have a metal characteristic and one of the mixed elements has to be a metal. Steel is a great example of an alloy since it is comprised of carbon and iron.

SUSPENSIONS

Suspensions are heterogeneous and are comprised of particles of a solid and a liquid, and the particles will not dissolve. When mixed together the particles are dispersed throughout the liquid. However, when left alone, the particles will settle. Mixing sand and water is a great example of a suspension.

Glass and bottle of milk

COLLOIDS

Colloids are heterogeneous and result when small particles of substance distribute evenly throughout another substance. While this may seem the same as a solution, its particles will remain suspended other than dissolving in the solution.

Milk is a terrific example of a colloid since its mixture of liquid butterfat is dispersed throughout the water and remains suspended. Even though they are known to mostly be heterogeneous, they can contain qualities of being homogeneous as well.

CHEMICAL REACTION

A chemical reaction occurs when substances undergo a change chemically to create a separate substance.

Rocket Space Ship

WHERE DO THEY OCCUR?

While you might think a chemical reaction only happens in a science lab, actually they are occurring in our ever day world, all the time. Any time you eat something, your body will use a chemical reaction in order to break the food into energy. Some additional example would be photosynthesis, batteries that produce electricity, burning wood, and rusting metal.

Have you ever seen a rocket lift-off in to space? They are propelled by a reaction occurring as liquid oxygen and liquid hydrogen are combined.

One reaction causing a sequence of reactions is often referred to as a chain reaction.

Melted ice cubes

As ice melts, it goes through a physical change from a solid to a liquid. This is not, however, a chemical reaction since it stays as the same physical substance (H_2O).

WHAT ARE REAGENTS, REACTANTS, AND PRODUCTS?

Reagents and reactants are those substances used to make a chemical reaction occur. The reactant is the substance consumed during a reaction.

A product is the substance produced by the chemical reaction.

Tubes with reagents

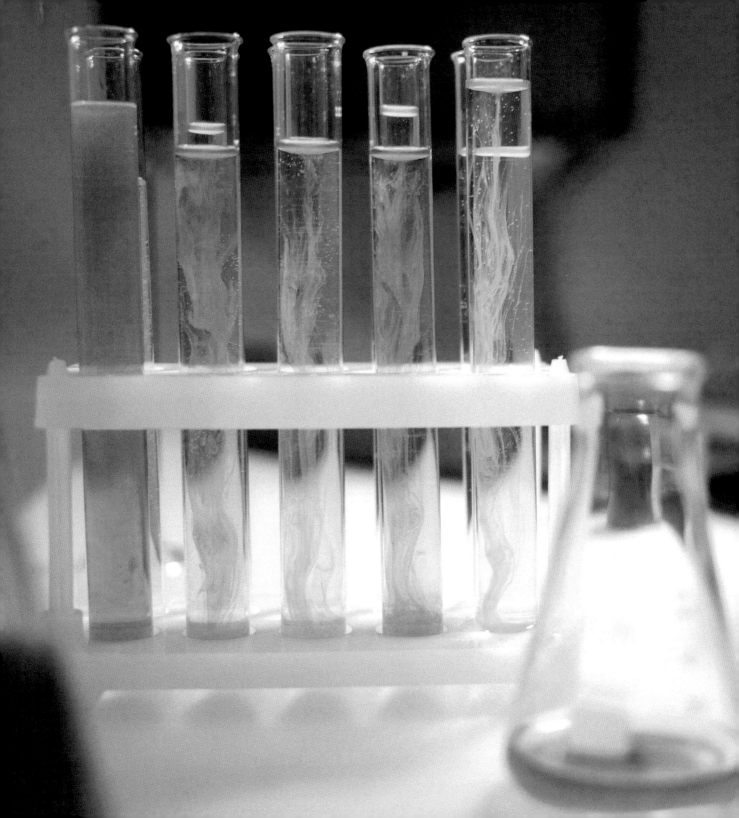

WHAT IS THE REACTION RATE?

Chemical do not all react at the same rate. Some will happen quickly, similar to an explosion, and others, like rusting metal, will take a longer amount of time. The reaction rate is the speed that a reactant turns into a product.

This rate can be altered by adding an energy such as electricity, sunlight, or heat. Adding an energy can cause the rate of the reaction to increase significantly. Another way to increase the reaction rate is by increasing the pressure or concentration of the reactants.

Solar panel, photovoltaic, alternative electricity source

Universal reactor work station with a
range of easily interchangeable vessels

WHAT ARE THE DIFFERENT TYPES OF REACTIONS?

There are several different forms of chemical reactions. Below are some examples:

SYNTHESIS REACTION – This is a reaction that occurs when two substances mix to create a new substance.

This is the equation: A + B $\longrightarrow$ AB.

DECOMPOSITION REACTION – This is a reaction that occurs when a complex substance is broken down and forms into two different substances.

This is the equation: AB $\longrightarrow$ A + B.

COMBUSTION – This is a reaction that occurs once oxygen mixes with a separate compound and forms carbon dioxide and water. Combustion reactions generate energy we know as heat.

SINGLE DISPLACEMENT – This reaction is also known as a substitute reaction. Think of this as a reaction when one of the compounds acquires a substance from a separate compound.

This is the equation: A + BC $\longrightarrow$ AC + B.

DOUBLE DISPLACEMENT - This reaction is also referred to as a metathesis reaction. Think of it as two separate compounds exchanging substances.

This is the equation: AB + CD $\longrightarrow$ AD + CB.

PHOTOCHEMICAL REACTION – This reaction involves photons obtained from light. An example of this kind of reaction is photosynthesis.

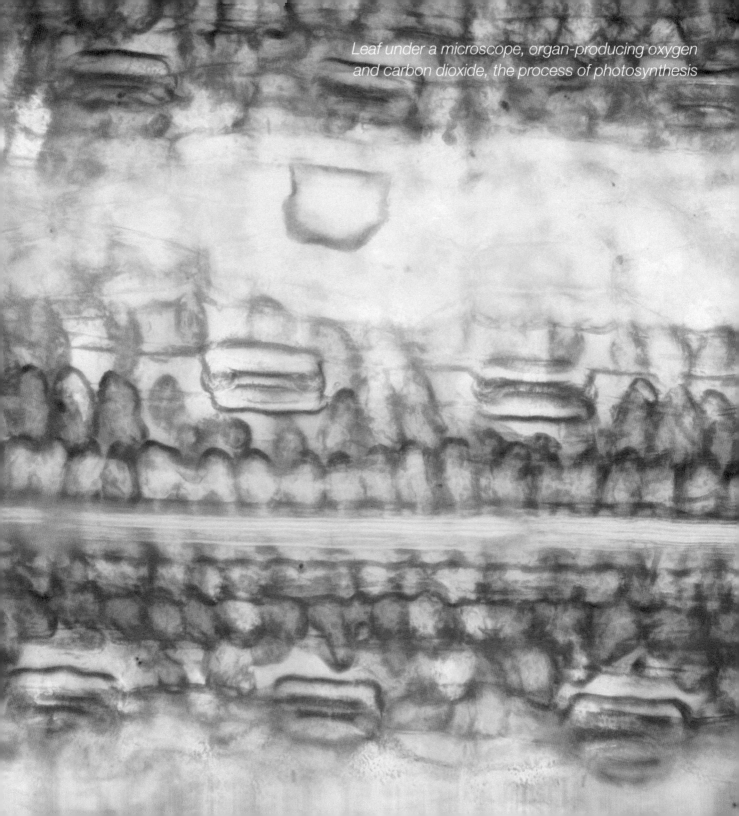

Leaf under a microscope, organ-producing oxygen and carbon dioxide, the process of photosynthesis

Charcoal that is smoking and burning on a grill

WHAT IS THE DIFFERENCE BETWEEN CATALYST AND INHIBITORS?

Occasionally, you might want to add a third substance to slow down or speed up a reaction. You can add a catalyst to assist with speeding up the rate of reaction. Differing from the other reagents, a catalyst is not utilized by the reaction. On the other hand, an inhibitor would be utilized to slow it down.

WHAT IS BONDING?

Our world consists of small units of matter that are referred to as atoms. Chemical bonding is the how the atoms stick together and form substances.

METHANOL HYDROGEN BONDING

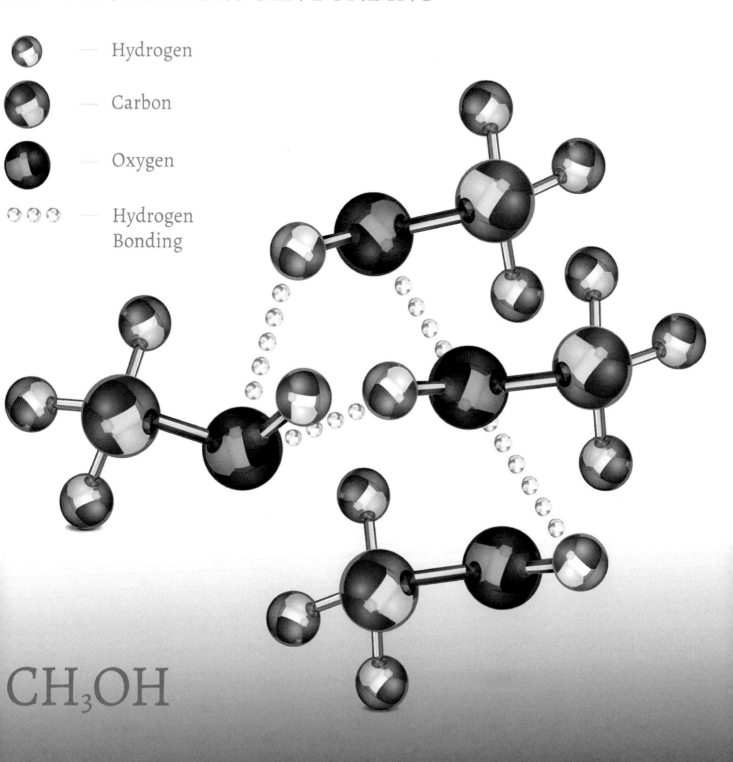

— Hydrogen

— Carbon

— Oxygen

— Hydrogen Bonding

CH_3OH

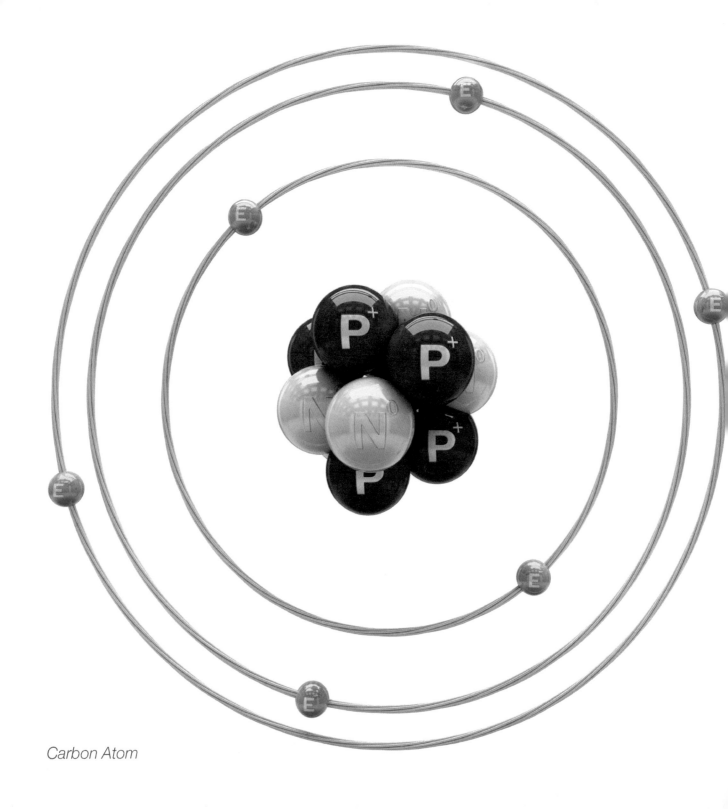

Carbon Atom

WHAT IS AN ATOM?

Every element consists of its unique atom made from a certain number of protons contained in its nucleus referred to as its atomic number. Each of these atoms also includes the same number of protons as it contains electrons. Atoms found in molecules stay together by the attraction between the shared electrons and the nucleus.

WHAT ARE THE ELECTRON SHELLS?

The atom's nucleus is orbited by its electrons. These electrons remain in layers which are known as shells. Each of the shells can contain only a certain amount of electrons: the first layer holds two, the second layer holds eight, the third layer holds eighteen, and so on.

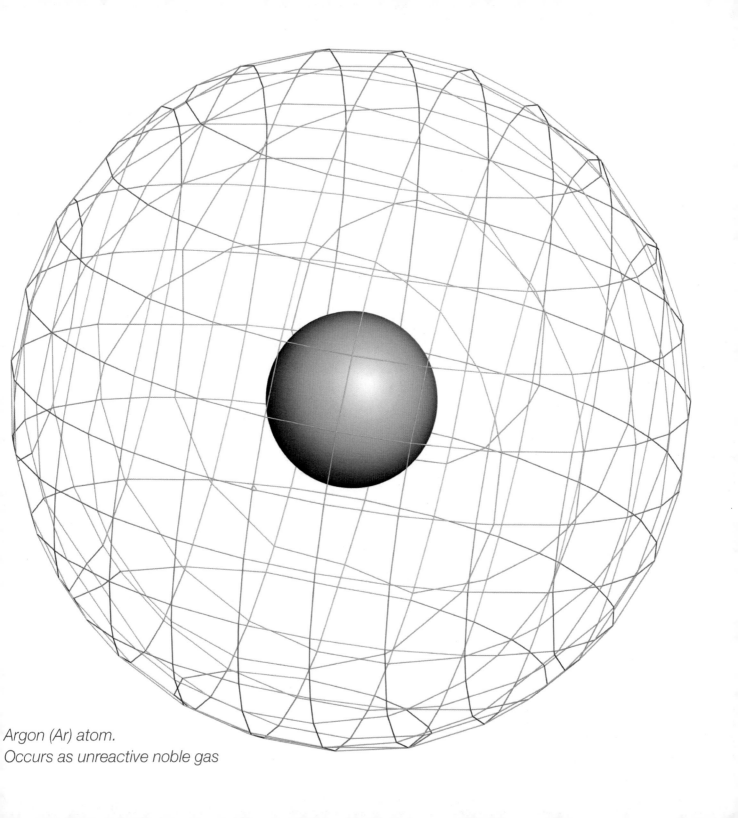

Argon (Ar) atom.
Occurs as unreactive noble gas

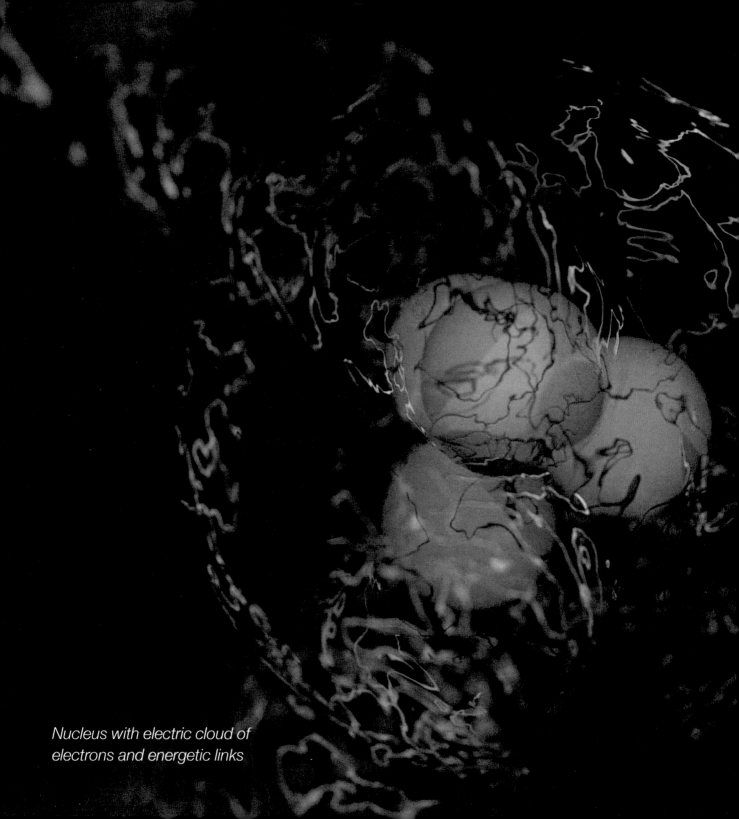

Nucleus with electric cloud of electrons and energetic links

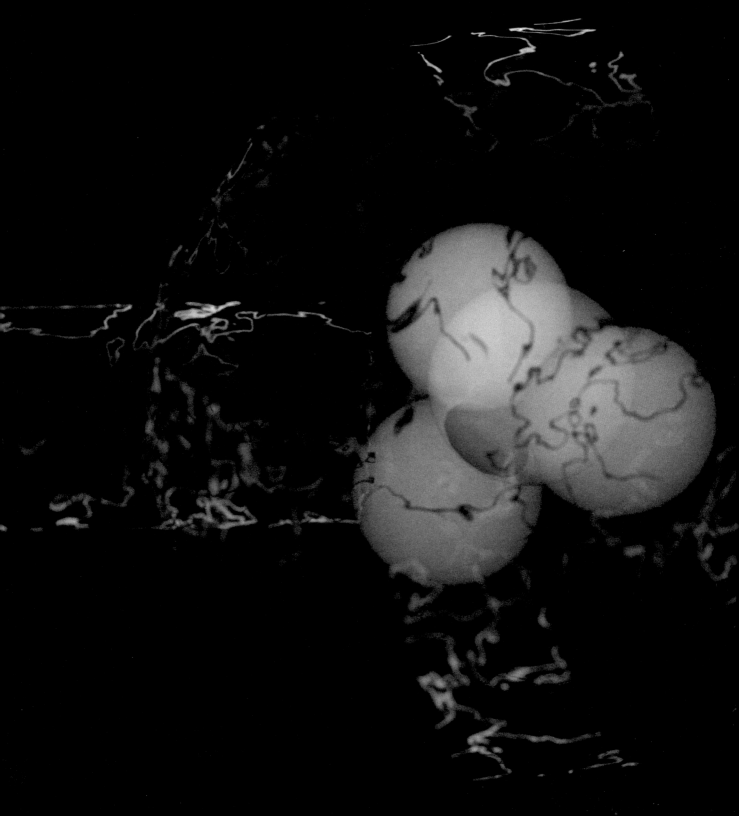

WHAT IS THE OUTER SHELL?

While all atoms desire a complete outer shell, the only elements that naturally have this complete outer shell are noble gases that fall to the right on the periodic table. Thus, as atoms that do not have a full outer shell encounter other atoms, they have an inclination to gain or give up electrons.

WHAT ARE VALENCE ELECTRONS?

Valence electrons are the number of electrons in an outer shell that can contribute to form bonds with other atoms. Atoms that have a relatively empty outer shell want to give away electrons. An example would be when an atom contains 1 electron out of 8 possible electrons in its outer shell, it wants to give up that electron so that the outer shell is full. Atoms containing a fairly full outer shell will want to add electrons to complete it. An example would be when an atom contains 6 out of 8 electrons in its outer shell, it will attempt to get 2 electrons so as to fill its outer shell.

CHEMICAL BONDING

Nonpolar covalent

Polar covalent

Ionic

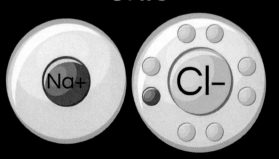

Metallic

Hydrogen

WHAT IS IONIC BONDING?

When one element gives an electron (electrons) to another element insuring that both elements now have a full outer shell this is known as ionic bonding. Ionic bonding occurs mostly between the metals which are located to the left of the periodic table.

WHAT IS COVALENT BONDING?

Covalent bonding occurs when atoms share electrons rather giving away or taking electrons, providing both elements with full outer shells. These electrons always share in pairs.

For additional information about these subjects, research the internet, go to your local library, and ask questions of your teachers, family, and friends.